Endearing Rhymes:
A-Z TV Shows

Wynette McKenzie

Publisher's Note: The poems in this book reference television shows in capital letters, but do not refer to the plot of the shows. The topics and content of the poems are fictional. All photographs are originally taken by the poet.

Endearing Rhymes: A-Z TV Shows ©
by Wynette McKenzie 2015

Photographs© by Wynette McKenzie

ISBN 978-1-941726-21-1

Five Little Angels Publishing.

All photographs by Wynette McKenzie.

Copyright 2015 by Five Little Angels, LLC.

A TV Shows (Day Dreaming)

I have an Absolutely Fabulous idea to create my version of All In The Family, please no screams!

A grand Adventure Time, not quite like Aladdin: A Musical Spectacular, but so far my American Dreams

All I ask of everyone is to be patient, do not query and try to ask Are We There Yet?

Or this might just become an Arrested Development on A.N.T. Farm and cause me to fret

So my theme will be simple, an American Dad married to America's Next Top Model, stop grinning!

Before it turns into an American Horror Story and certainly not a single person will be winning

Their children Austin & Ally are Almost Heroes but not there so far, they hooked up with Alf today

Seemingly, even though he is Almost Human, he moved next door to the Army Wives anyway

Are You Being Served so far? Maybe not! My friend Alley McBeal offered an idea from faraway

She said since Alvin and the Chipmunks are all grown up, they should become Agents of S.H.I.E.L.D.

Protecting the Animaniacs from the Angel Beasts with the Aqua Teen Hunger Force in the field

Apparently! They can form an Alias with the American Dragon Andromeda, Okay! Not looking good

Arthur the spy next door is pretending to be Andy Barker P.I, when he is really a wimp from the hood

He views the Andy Griffith Show and Avatar: The Last Airbender looking like an Awkward Axe Cop

Accidentally On Purpose views the Atom Ant Show, acting somewhat ordinary, nothing like a cheap shot

While his brother is constantly disturbing the peace, asking his cousin Archer to jump on the roof

Yelling Auf Wiedersehen Pet, peeking in the gap screaming Are You There Chelsea? This is not About A Boy, What a spoof!

With all these distractions, I hope I do not need Anger Management; all I can say is that I am no Angel and this American Family story

Departed right where it all got started on the Antiques Roadshow then Ashes to Ashes! Sorry I tried, but not to your glory

B TV Shows in Rhymes (Envisioning)

My Brothers And Sisters, you are all Breaking Bad, planning to go to Beverly Hills 90210 to pry

Superficially, with the Big Shots showing off their eyeglasses through their cunning Brass Eye

Since most of them have formed a Band of Brothers from Boston Public, Just don't ask me why!

Instead of being Barney and Friends; The Bold and The Beautiful, It has become more like Beauty and the Beast

Apparently not like the Black Donnellys, where Being Human is normal to say the least

For now, make believe that this could become a Battlestar Galactica of Beauty and the Geek

I'm no Braniac! This group is Berserk, driving me to the Bottom of Buzz Lightyear Star Command creek

They not only assembled the Boston Legal Team and Babylon 5 crew, but started Beast Wars

Beside Batman plus Beavis and Butt-Head they formed Blue Bloods like Bridezilla and their files were discovered

The Bogan Hunters seized them using a Black Ladder from Barney Miller's forbidden drawers

Now the luxury Board Walk Empire that consist of famous Bob's Burger has relocated to the Boondocks

It will be managed by Bill Nye, The Science Guy who was so intelligent, but is now bewitched

If this is their version of Big Love, I guess Birds of Feather do flock together with the Black Butler

Opening his Black Books of Bones to of course, what do you think? You guessed it, snitched!

Back to the Barnyard with Bananaman, where Being Erica is where Boy Meets World with Blue Heelers

The Big Bang Theory is to Beware of Becker pretending to be Blake's 7 Brady Bunch with big wheelers

If you look closely Bunheads, there is a Burn Notice, warning us to be like the Ben 10 Group

Unlike the Biggest Loser, try to Bleach the Bridge to Brotherhood like the Boys over Flowers troop

I'm no Bionic Woman or Buffy the Vampire Slayer, but envision this plan and you will be Better off Ted

C TV Shows in Rhymes (Impressing)

I am not charmed by your idea of Camelot Curious George: first off it is very early in the morning!

Taking me to the Chappelle's Show on a Coach Ride to Cougar Town, as if I am desperate and yearning

Flashback! It feels like we're going to Clone High with cheap seats designed by Count Duckula Chuck

Feeling more like the Chaser's War on Everything! Featured on Charlie Rose Case Closed, I am not to be mocked

This is more resembling The Chip and Dale Rescue Rangers fighting Chicago Fire, while hanging out with Cow and Chicken

So Curb Your Enthusiasm, and get ready for a good The Colbert Report Code Lyoke tongue licking

I envisioned a Crayon Skin Chan on China Beach in the Chalk Zone with The CSI Miami class

In its place I'm with Clark and Michael of Code Nabie, staging Criminal Minds with Corner Gas

Since seeing Cowboy Behop on Chelsea Lately, I learned that Colombo is not a Caveman Community

Your hint of a Castle on Carnation Street is like Crossing Jordon with Courage the Cowardly Dog in unity

So quit the Crusade playing Cupid in Cougar Town, it's more like The Cleveland Show minus the laughter

I will surely have a Carnivore in my Creature Comforts backyard, seeing the Care Bears Nation hereafter

D TV Show in Rhymes (Paradise)

Silence! I told you from Day One Drake and Josh, and also featured on Dish Nation, there are no Duck Tales there

The Dukes of Hazzard and Dr. Quinn Medicine Woman are Drawn Together as Duel Masters of care

The Daily Show here will be Dead Ringers of Disney's Adventures of the Gummi Bears

No Signs of Dirty Jobs or any Dumbo earning Dirty Sexy Money with soundless fears

Surprisingly, there are no Dark Shadows resembling Davinci's Demons out and around

The streets are paved with pure gold and flowing into Dawson's Creek with a beautiful sound

The Doctors Dr. Seuss and Dr. Who; will not prescribe any medications to the Desperate Housewives

Unless they can repair the damages they caused at The Dragon Ball ruining everyone's lives

All the Dinosaurs of Donkey Kong Country will eventually be Dead Wood and turned to Dirt

Replenished and transformed, forming precious jewels and stones on a jasper wall in a new earth

All can build a Doll House, not being afraid of Dad's Army on the Drew Carey Show hall of fame

Dr. Phil should have already solved everyone's problems and Due South with the Duck Dodgers again

No time for that sign in Durarara!! that says "Do Not Disturb"

It will be so peaceful that Danny Phantom and Deion's Family will be blissful, and grateful they were gifted to absorb

Dexter whispered that Dilbert will be singing and sounding like a Darkwing Duck

No Death Note will be left by anyone trying to get a ransom so good luck!

Dharma & Greg will not require a Dragnet to Drive, since they will have wings

Please warn Doogie Houser, MD of the Dark Angel in Disguise that plays with Doug things

She states that if you want to be "Dead Like Me in Deep Space Nine", just flirt!

You do not need Dave The Barbarian to play Danger Mouse with Dilbert

Please try not to miss the boat to paradise and be in the Deep End, so be alert!

E TV Shows in Rhymes (Adoration)

The Extras blog posted a question; it asked do you know why Everybody Hates Chris?

It beats me, but the answer is on Extra, so tune in, you don't want to miss

I confirmed on The Ellen DeGeneres Show, they said it's because Everybody Loves Raymond on the Eastwick bliss

Ed, Edd, N Eddy agreed that it was not until the Eleventh Hour that everyone selected him

Eli Stone vexed to Encourage him, that fitting in, is ridding himself of his Elementary ways within

Eek! the Cat is also not fond of him; he prefers to stay Eastbound & Down with Empire around

The Exosquad from Eastwick also agreed, now this is not cool, since they are all in his town

Well, Earthworm Jim is planning a reunion of all Chris's friends at Earth 2 skating blitz

He would like everyone to invite all his friends and relatives, but nobody from The Ex List

Eerie Indiana will be the host and the Eureka and Eureka Seven drama club will be performing

The Event was a blast, no ER reports, Chris was loved and behaviors just started transforming

No more Even Stevens, by Evening Shade all attitudes had an Extreme makeover Emergency!

Remember love is patient and kind. The cast of Empire, Eve, Eli Stone and Eight is Enough heard from the Early Edition show and responded with much urgency

F TV Shows in Rhymes (Tolerance)

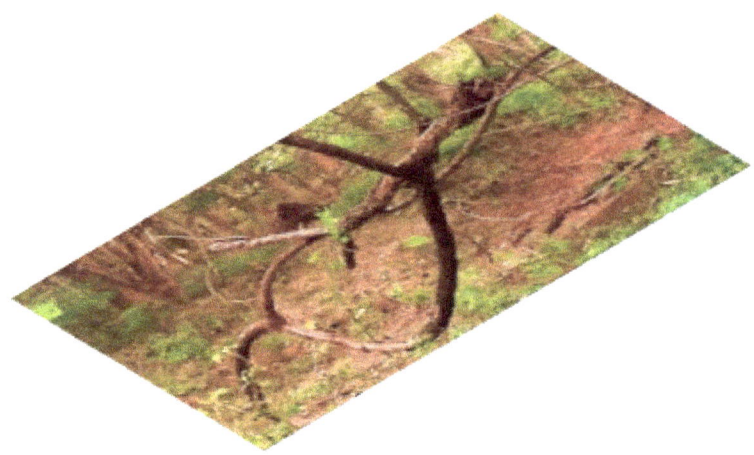

While the world needs more love, try to live like Flex and Shanice, we don't have to wait for Falling Skies

Or the Flintstones to remind us of the Fawlty Towers near The Foster's Food Paradise

Unity begins On Friday The 13th, Ferb Speaks at the Futurama Face Off about love For Better Or Worse and the Facts Of Life

The topics will be on Family Matters, mainly how to avoid a Family Feud without strife

Other issues will include stabilizing Family Fortunes, and eluding the Filty Rich Catflap

Father Ted and the Football Wives will speak on the Foster's Home For Imaginary Friends mishap

Franklin & Bash and Friends from Flavor Of Love will give out tickets to Fantasy Island

On Fridays there will be Friday Night Lights at the Fushigi Yuugi Fishtronaut club in the sand

The Freaks and Geeks will team up with the Fresh Prince of Bel-Air for a Freakazoid brunch

A Flash Forward, this is all Fairly Legal, as long as there's no Full House in the Fastlane at lunch

Lots of Free Stuff! Like Fish Hooks, Fruits Basket, and a Fringe book from Frasier

The Flintstones will present the top prizes, a Frisky Dingo trophy, a gold Firefly and a Family Guy eraser

All done as a tribute to The Forgotten crew of The Flight of the Conchords and Flight 2 F-troops

Felicity of the FLCL will do our closing speech on tolerance, I hope that everyone took something away from this event that enriched your life, the night's Flash Point for all groups

G TV Shows in Rhymes (Admonishing)

According to the Genealogy Roadshow I have Great Expectations of visiting Gilligan's Island, and certainly living The Good Life

For now, I must anticipate on being Glee, and learning how to be The Good Wife

Oh Goodness Gracious Me, I am not like the Great Teacher Onizuta who lives in The Golden Palace

Good Morning Washington recounted that he watches and studies every episode of Grey's Anatomy every night with his darling wife Alice

His student George Lopez and his children Gavin & Stacey will be starring in an episode of Gunsmoke

It's time I just Get Smart and learn the rules of the Game of Thrones, because losing is just no joke

I'm trying to fit in this Gimme Gimme Gimme world of imitating the Gilmore Girls and their Green Wing

It sounds Grim & Evil but avoid a Gossip Girl or being Grounded For Life, because that's an evil thing

Good Luck Charlie if you see Greg the Bunny because Good Moring America reported that you became like a Ghost in the Shell

If Gravity Falls I will be rehearsing for the Broadway show Gundam Wing, but only time will tell

I will settle now for an outing with Garfield and friends at their playhouse on Gintama Street

There's a Grimm gamble, a new spin off of The Golden Girls will soon debut, so get your hot seat

The cast of The Game and Gargoyles are also having a party at Galactica for all G.I. Joe Extreme fans

I'm no Guinevere Jones, but I will be at the Greek café with my Goof Troop Gundam SEED and clans

Now by this time next year, God's willing I should have accomplished something, and no time for Generation Kill

H TV Shows in Rhymes (Development)

I'm deciding if I should be Home and Away for my big Home Improvement to a high rise

In the meantime I'm keeping up with Hot in Cleveland, except my version portrayed on History Detectives was cold in Columbia in a House of Lies

The whole idea of moving to Holby City resembles Homicide, Life on the Streets with Heroes pills

Happy Days are gone and I need some H20: Just Add Water to make this Hell's kitchen, a Hometime paradise of The Hills

Harvey Birdman, Attorney At Law reminded me, it will take a while, so I should not get Hysteria, Really! Oh now the drama begins, start playing the band!

I'm hoping my Heroes, Herman's Head and Hercules will go with me on a House Hunters tour of Hawaii Five-O Homeland

Now I understand, How to Make it in America and not be Hyperdrive on the Homefront,

I really need to stay cool in the Hidden Hills, unlike Horrid Henry, teaching How Not To Live Your Life, so blunt!

Have I got News For You, Hercules, the Legendary Journey and Hex are now Head of the Class!

Their new boss Hamish Macbeth promoted them in a Heartbeat and that was their ticket to Hennessey in Hollyoaks, not so Fast!

It was publicized that a Horatio Hornblower name Hamtaro discovered their Highway To Heaven; It was in the Hands of Hope and Faith

Hey Dude! You Human Giant, it was written in your Hidden Palms, and were tattered as you were Halfway Home near Happy Tree Friends gate

I must stay strong like History's Strongest Disciple: Kenichi, who fought Hogan's Heroes in his House

I will be staying at Hotel Hell, watching How I Met Your Mother repeats, sneaking like a diminutive mouse

Hannah Montana is no longer Hanging with Mr. Cooper in Hannibal

She became a new fan of Here Comes Honey Boo Boo, now that she became a quiet gal

While I am waiting like the Hellcats for my new Haven, I'll be watching Hancock's Half Hour

Hoping I won't get the Hill Street Blues, I will dream of my version of Hitchhikers Guide to the Galaxy with super power

Hey Arnold! Why in the world did you decide to use me as a Human Target?

You should have recycled the Hetalia-Axis Powers at Hollywood 7 where you had a fling with Margaret

By the way my friend HawthoRNe, who is a Head Case, has decided to marry Hank and move to Happy Town

Her job transfer caused her to leave Harper's Island, Wow! Still stuck with Hi Hi Puffy Ami Yumi, but so much peace, now that she's no longer around

So although it's a continuous Hustle, I will resort to seeing Home Movies of The Honeymooners

Though I'm no Human Giant, patience is a virtue, so I will cruise around in my Highlander, praying and wishing for Happy Endings, that this home project will finish a lot sooner

I TV Shows in Rhymes (Subsistence)

Guess what? I Survived a Japanese Game Show, In Living Color and lived to tell about it

I became an Instant Star and Intelligence played a part, but I was with The It Crowd like the Icons; featured on The Insider what a good fit!

Just in case Inspector Gadget comes around, evenhandedly say I am In Treatment and not In Plain Sight because I am a Weasel that loves to squeal

It's a miracle that It's Always Sunny In Philadelphia, because Inspector Morse and Invader Zim thinks that this is not Ideal

Ironically, I love you, even though I Love New York, I'll Fly Away to discover If Loving You is Wrong and the meaning of Invasion America with Inuyasha

My Infinite Stratos is to send Inspector Rex on Inside Edition where I Spy on the In Living Color cast with my buddy Stasha

The It Factor here is to be like The Invisible Man, not The Invaders crashing everything

Draw up a plan and acquire the art of cooking like the Iron Chef, also learning survival skills similar to Iron Man undertaking something

Don't be like The Inbetweeners, dreaming all day long saying, I Dream of Jeannie and I Love Lucy; they may need Iyanla Fix My Life in a short span

They are just trying hard to be comparable to Insomniac with Dave Attel crying out "I'm with her," all you need is a solid back up plan

J TV Shows in Rhymes (Bliss)

My new TV show version of John and Kate Plus 8 will be long coming but I guarantee it will be very humble

If it does not work out Just Shoot me! No please don't! Just kidding, so you won't have to see Judge Mathis, I do not want The Jetsons empire to crumble

So my cast will be Jake 2.0, Jake and the Fat Man, Jake and the Never Land Pirates, just forget it! Too many Jakes and company, I'm starting over, this time Johnny Bravo will pick the lucky cast

As long as it does not resemble the cast of The Jetsons, or this Jamie Kennedy Experiment will not be Justified and will soon become a heavy task

An update John Doe is stressing that he will bring in Joyce and The Wheeled Warriors, if this is really true

The new show's lawyers Jeeves & Wooster PA and Judge Judy will stress that the contract should not include Jimmy Neutron or or they will have to sue

Hahaha did I just laugh? Is this Judge Faith, by all means you can also feature it on The Jeff Foxworthy Show

Because John From Cincinnati has a plan of attack, to send Joan Of Arcadia to investigate all of the allegations before it becomes the new Journey Man and Johnny Quest whistle blow

Onward with the cast please! This leaves Jessie, Jag, Jpod, Jeky11, Jake and Bobby, Johnny Quest, and Johnny Test and Joey as this will be set in the town of Jericho

So you might say well done! But not for me, unless I was on the Jersey Shore with Jakers! The Adventures of Piggley Winks, this is not in my Justice League and will drive me up Jonathan Creek

Now, J. O. A. N. A. S and John Adams agrees, this just made me look like a Jackass on Jimmy Kimmel Live; and now I'm through and going to sleep

K TV Shows in Rhymes (SURPRISE)

The Larry King Special Report will have an extraordinary broadcast, that Winter Wonderland of Kingwood Country is having a community block party

Please be prepared to invite everyone in and around the community including Kath & Kim and Marty

It will be grander than Keeping up with the Kardashians, so magnificent it will be called The Killing

Just shout and whistle at anyone you see in the Kingdom of Knots Landing and all who are willing

Precautions will be taken to make sure the King of Queens is protected and Karen Sisco will not be Kidnapped by Keen Eddie again as a sign

Kid Nation, adult's station detectives will be on patrol ensuring that all will be safe as the party guests begin to unwind

Kath and Kim are the party's hostesses and will be safeguarding everyone that attends, all will have a chance to win one of 100 tickets to see Kung Fu Panda: Legends of Awesomeness, all free!

Key & Peele will end the party with a chance for the two show's queens to win a date with the Knight Rider Kyle XY Kings, Oh how glee!

Kudlow and Company will have parting gifts for everyone; soon this will be all past, and no more part of my Kurau Phantom Memory, just endure and you will see

L TV Shows in Rhymes (Education)

Larry King Special will debut a new show; A Life Unexpected, is the title of a new experiment, the Law & Order Trial by Jury will be launching.

It will be a seven-part series, this research will consist of the lifecycle of several individuals and their Life On Mars

This Less Than Perfect experiment will began at Laguna Beach but will not include The League or A-List stars

Laverne and Shirley will be the first guide of series one, in The Lone Gunmen Township of the Loop, east side of mars studying on The Life and Times of Juniper Lee

While Little Miss Jocelyn will be the second guide of series two in the La Femme Nikita township of Lil Bush, west side of mars, studying The Life and Times of Tim who is now starring on Glee

Although this will be a very tedious series of studies, The Looney Tunes Show, Lilo & Stich and Lucky Louie will be shown on satellite television for recreation time

Louis and Clark will be the third guide of series three, in Little Mosque on the Prairie township of Las Vegas, north side of mars, studying the Life of Ryan, who lived his Life on a Stick just fine

Ironically our choice for the fourth guide to series four, created The Latest Buzz because it was Louie, since he refused to use The L word thinking that he will create a Lipstick Jungle of The Lying Game,

However they agreed to be partial and Love American Style, as well as not be like a Lonesome Dove similar to Lupin the Third on The Loop house of fame

While this entire experiment will be featured on The Larry Sanders Show, Life with Derek will be postponed for some Leverage and Law and Order in Little Britain transitory

Evenhandedly, the Legend of Zelda will also resume at its regular time following Lincoln Heights. Look Around You for a Lost Girl, but please turn her in to The Lone Gunmen because it was discovered that she is Lucky, the daughter of the Devil, so it will be mandatory

Laurel and Hardy will be the fifth guide to series five the Legend of the Seeker township of Lexx, south side of mars, studying the Life of Ryan, who Love Hina on The Love Boat

The Legend of Tarzan crew will be the sixth guide to series six, beneath the mars layers, studying, in Leave It to Beaver township of Luther, studying the Life of Louie who imitated Love Thy Neighbor to stay afloat

Well the seventh guide and the last of this series will be a special on The Late Show with Craig Ferguson and it will be featured from a Little House on The Prairie, while this may sound unexciting,

Look Around You; Do you see anything more interesting? Okay then! Stick with the program and don't Lie to Me and most of all, do not get Lost, just think of this as something quite beguiling

M TV Shows in Rhymes (Prerequisites)

Even though I am Married with Children, I must let you know about my Magical Project 5. You see, there are five girls but no boys so My So-called Life and Modern Family will soon be debuting on MythBusters unfolds

My Mission Hill is to study Mrs. Browns Boys, hoping it will not be the Mock of the Week. So eager for My three Sons, I am dreaming of Mystic Knights Of Tir Na Nog.

It is My World and Welcome to It, It may sound Mental but at least you've been told

Murder She Wrote! Said Murphy Brown, how can she dare when she is friends with Mona The Vampire. Melissa and Joey thinks the idea sounds like Midsomer Murders, Whatever!

She and Joey are not Masters of Sex, they love Moonlighting in the Moonlight only to Make it or Break it at Melrose Place.

I will try to be jolly like Maid Marian and Her Merry Men, but from MacGyver point of view, she loves Mad Men demanding them saying "Marry Me" but pretends to have a smiling face

Martin and Merlin gave me a solid lecture on the Man To Man With Dean Learner Show. They stated that it would be a Miami Vice situation like The Mentalist on Magnum P. I.

Matlock also called to say it would be the Most Hated Family In America, I Wonder why?

Well he insisted it would look like Monty Python's Flying Circus, with The Monkees looking like Misfits pretending to be Mighty Morphin Power Rangers spies

Enough already! I need to have a Mind of Mencia and play The Match Game with Malcolm & Eddie on Malibu Shores and just put on My Sassy Girl Mama's Family disguise face

This is now sounding like a Metalocalypse with The Mighty B! on Mutant High. A rendition of Men Behaving Badly and Men in Trees, so please Mary Hartman, Mary Hartman! Help me to have a backup plan in place.

I am My Own Worst Enemy, My family call me a Master Chef but I am only a M. A. S. K. from The Mask Animated every Mayday.

The Mystery Science Theater 3000 will feature My Life as a Teenage Robot along with My Little Pony, so please join me whether you are Married Single Other.

Matlock has referred me to a shrink called Maria-Sama ga Miteru because this story of my sons is now like Man Vs Wild reminiscent of The Man Show, It will be introduced on Mad TV.

Well the McLeod's Daughters have some faith in me waiting for My Boys, well! I thought so until I heard them telling Mr. Bean that I am insane and nobody should even bother

If everyone thinks I am the Mentalist and part Monk with no Moral Orel, I will just call a Mannix from The Mindy Project and request a Monkey instead.

I will depart from the presence of The Munsters for a much deserve vacation at the Miami7 hotel in M*A*S*H County

Marvin Marvin from Marb and the Magic Movie Machine called saying "Girl I am Mad About You." What a load of Mutant X, more like Murder One.

He sent in another fool with no class proclaiming My Name Is Earl, It could be Moone boy for all I care, looking like Monster Allergy from the Musketeers.

Can someone play Miss Match on The Meredith Vieira Show if they do not Minder? The Middle cast will be judges along with Megam NT Warrior.

So much for My Spy Family, I think they need a Medium! One name comes to my mind, Moesha because she is their peer

My Favorite Martin is to Mucha Lucha! Like a Mistress at Meerkat Manor where I can unwind and watch Mork and Mindy, Montell Williams and The Muppets Tonight shows.

I desire to be laughing and forgetting all about Mr. Show who got this all started in the first place, leaving the moral of this story wanting to have sons, as The Mrs. Bradley Mysteries unsolved.

Well see all of you at Monarch of The Glen resorts in My Mother the Car Country Club eating catered meals from Michael Kitchen, Cheers!

N TV Shows in Rhymes (Caution)

While watching The New Adventures Of Old Christine on the television show NCIS, I was shocked to find out that My Nice Friends Ned and Stacey from The New Yankee Workshop were The New Statesman original Night Stalker

The New Avengers from Nashville from The No 1 Ladies Detective Agency are on the case at Night Court. Nurse Jackie from New Amsterdam was asked to monitor their vital signs, since she is The New Girl at The News Radio, and somewhat a feisty talker

Reporter Ni Hao Kai-Lan will be in The Newsroom keeping us posted on any updates in the case, it will be shown late but Not the Nine O'clock News, since this will be too much Northern Exposure

The NYPD Blue station stated that this is No Ordinary Family, more like a Ninja Warrior from North and South who were Neighbors to Naruto so now we all need some closure

Newhart and Naturally Sadie will be training everyone with Ned's Declassified School Survival Guide. This training will avert anything like this from happening.

Nikita is worried, since her Nanny has to travel alone along the same path where they stalked and Nip/Tuck.

So there is a new billboard in the streets saying "Not Going Out" delight in stay indoors, or you will be Numb3rs at Newport Harbor. Is this scaring you? It should!

So be aware, and Never Mind The Buzzrocks, just listen to NCIS: Los Angeles radio station for the verdict and good luck

O TV Shows in Rhymes (Failure)

Once Upon A Time I had One Foot in The Grave, because I was Out Of Control and my sins Outnumbered the length of October Road.

It took the entire cast of The OC to get me back in One Piece. I had several One On One visits with the Doctors of Oz in an Off Center that was Open All Hours to convey my load

The Office made it clear that Ozzy & Onx from the Odd Job bank were The Originals, until they heard of me. Ah! The Odd Couple could not pull off that One Tree Hill stunt

Back to me, since Orange Is The New Black, I signed up for Oprah's Master Class to accomplish Operation change but in just a split second I thought I was 2 Fat 2 Fly and flunked the entire lesson.

I picked up the pieces at this instant, Once And Again I registered for Oprah's Life Class but did not have the strength to endure. I was eventually featured on Oprah Where Are They Now?

I was the honored guest of The Oprah Winfrey Show entitled Only Fools And Horses, how sad! But at least I confessed, and did not sugar coat it, how blunt!

P TV Shows in Rhymes (Witty)

Let's try being Politically Incorrect, first nobody has Perfect Hair Forever or have always lived with Picket Fences, Well maybe! The Privileged, but most of us live like The Pretender while on the inside we are always upset

Some of us have to make a Prison Break from Pets TV, with the Press Gang, while others are Pretty Little Liars but Pride and Prejudice make us like a Predator Fail and a Prime Suspect

The Philanthropist in some of us helps us to remember our ancestors from the Past Life while more or less of us just Party Down at the Peep Show and watch Pee-Wee's Playhouse being Penny Dreadful like Pinky and The Brain

Parenthood reminds nearly all of us that a Party of Five or more is no Point Pleasant or Peg Plus Cat, but a constant reminder of Pain Killer Jane and may just drive some insane

A few of us try to resort to a Prehistoric Park on a Prehistoric Planet in your dreams, if you can pull the Press Your Luck stunt.

Plik Plock some People Like Us have to dream of meeting The Prince Of Tennis, while others dream of a get-together with Princess Tutu but they eventually get Punk'd

Approximately, a few of us would rather Profit on Pound Puppies in Philly, how Psych! While others daydream of Pushing Daisies on Project Runway, discovering they were just Pulling a lot of Pucca junk

A number of us like Pepper Ann dream of owning The Penguins of Madagascar instead, drove you to become a Person of Interest in The Pacific

The Parks and Recreation will hold a Primeval concert featuring The Persuaders and if The Price is Right, It should be Packed To The Rafters. The guest stars are Peter Kay's Phoenix Nights Band, Pokémon, The Powerpuff Girls, Power Rangers: Ninja Storm, and Pac man and the Ghostly Adventure crew. They should all be so terrific

What more do you want? Don't be greedy before I have to assign Punky Brewster to a Private Practice for a Pair of Kings to judge all of you

My Perception of all this, is that we are all Perfect Strangers trying to survive in a Phineas and Ferb world, all around The Pillars of The Earth using The Powers of Matthew Star, so visit the town of Pacific Blue and try to continue to be true

Q TV Shows in Rhymes (Absurdity)

As cold as this may seem, in my Quarterlife it was just Quincy M.E and you said it me!

We took the Quantum Leap like a Quack Pack going Quark on the Street, trying to be all we can be

But Queer Eye for the Straight Guy tried to command me to listen to what he had to say

Well he was soft spoken and my hearing impaired self -did not hear what he had to say, so I conveyed it my own way

He came back a second time speaking in a louder voice saying I was Queer as Folk

Oh don't worry he was just making me laugh and that was his solitary overworked joke

R TV Shows in Rhymes (Transformation)

I need a ReBoot and be Reborn by faith, before Revolutionary Girl Utena take over. Relativity, I really should try to stay on the Right Path to Recovery on the Right side of Kansas, where Rachael Ray resides

First I must start by Raising the Bar by tracing my Roots and learn the Rules of Engagement. Rob and Big once said that Royal Pains starts from within. You do not have to hit a Redwall like The Raccoons in the Real World to abide

Randall and Hopkirk (Deceased) left us a valuable lesson that Revenge only brings Ramsey's Kitchen Nightmares to The Rockford Files

By Raising Hope your life will become Rainbow Bright and you will create a Revolution like The Royle Family of Rizzoli & Isles

Robot & Monster of The Real Adventures of Jonny Quest was featured on Raw Reality with Gail Kasper for a reason; this Raw Toonage will enable us to access Radio Free Roscoe

Rab C. Nelson said Raising Dad at the Roundhouse is driving him Rookie Blue, but Rupert his brother from Rebus is assisting him in buying a Roger Ramjet wheelchair to help him to be on the go

He needs more Rocket Power and a pretty darn good Rock Profile instead of sitting around like a Red Dwarf in a Robotech world of Ringer

Please Rescue Me from Rick and Monty wretched melodies, before I feature them on The Ren and Skimpy Show or Real Time with Bill Maher, they are hurting my ear drums pretending to be famous singers

My gut instinct tells me to just call Reno 911 in Rove to send the Robot Chicken to Rome because they are just creating Robot Wars in Roswell pretending to be Roommates trained by a band player

Rick and Monty said their best bet is to just Runaway! Before Rosanne and her Road Rovers show up during Recess, then it will seriously be Red V Blue

The Reaper propelled Richie Rich and Reba from Remington Steele to be a Rubicon and a modern day Robin Hood In RahXehon, to teach us how to live Rocko's Modern Life like Rudy Bloom in Raising Whitley and be true, not Ranma ½ but creating a whole new you

S TV Shows in Rhymes (Pleasurable)

Contrasting Survival of the Weirdest, My Side Order of life is to spend The Secret Saturdays worshipping in the Sanctuary

Learn The Starter Wife guide to Saving Grace by being The Shield to The Supernatural, not like a Star Wars Rebel or Sonny with a Chance adversary

So You Think You Can Dance, but do not Salute Your Shorts yet, because Sailor Moon and Sam & Cat were Saved By The Bell before a Soap and Soul Eater Scandal

Sit Down & Shut Up you Scorpion, before Stargate Universe start to Shake It Up! With the Savages and Scrubs on Sea Patrol in their sandal

The Sealab 2021 will make a slight Sea Change in Swington and the Schoolhouse Rock! Band will be featured on Shark Tank

I bet my Shooting Stars that Samantha Who? will be the new Shah of Sunset queen just to improve her Sleepy Hollow rank

Please allow me to use a Sledge Hammer to tap into Space: Above and Beyond in Smallville, so Scarecrow and Mrs. King don't sell her Sex and The City tapes to The Saddle Club bank

The Secret Life of the American Teenager is not the teenager of Sonny with a Chance. They use Samurai Pizza Cats as a disguise to enter the Samurai X to see Sabrina The Teenage Witch in the dark

While I attended a meeting in Swingtown, I heard that The Sons of Tucson and Southland played at South Park

The Sarah Jane Adventures was also featured at Shelley Duvall's Faerie Tale Theatre in Shinzo where Scooby Doo constantly tries to bark

Just before I go Six Feet Under I would like to Shuffle! All the Silver Spoons featured on Seinfeld like a Sheep in a Big City but certainly not on Sesame Street with a Spaced out Shark

Seth MacFarlane's Cavalcade of Cartoon Comedy will have its annual show at the Seaquest DSV country club; his honored guests will be Saint Seiya, Scryed, and Sanford and Son

This will take place on Saturday Night Live, with Seinfeld and Sherlock as the Sonic X host, The Show Biz show with David Spade will host the follow up event, what a Shuffle! of fun

Tickets are now available at the Studio 60 on the Sunset Strip and Studio Heights High. Other locations are at the Silver Wing café, Super Mario World lounge and the Sonic Underground theatre

There will be a host of events every hour. Below are the calendar of events and times to be your guide for the occasion. Starting at 12:00 p.m. and ending at 8:00 p.m., Sifi and Olly will be your presenters, the Squidbillies negotiator.

12:00 p.m. ----------Super Natural, Strangers with Candy with Skunk Boy at the Sweeny (Location 1)

1:00 p.m.------------SmackDown! Wrestling hosted by Smash at the Smash Lab (Location 2)

2:00 p.m.------------Stillgame hosted by the Storm Hawks at the Striperella (Location 3)

3:00 p.m.-------------Sports Night, hosted by Spike Milligan at the Squidbillies (Location 4)

4:00 p.m.-------------Starwars epic center, hosted by Special Unit 2 at the Spin City corner (Location 5)

5:00 p.m.-------------Spyder Games, hosted by The Spectacular Spiderman at The Suite Life on Land junction (Location 6)

6:00 p.m.--------------Space Cases, hosted by Space 1999 at the Splatalot division (Location 7)

7:00 p.m.--------------Speed Racer hosted by Street Hawk at the Street Fury shop (Location 8)

8:00 p.m.---------------Street Sounds Music Video Show hosted by Super Robot Monkey Team hyperforce Go! At the Supah Ninjas Club (Location 9)

Immediately after these events, if you are Still Standing and not Stoked, Oh that is So Random! There will be a Spawn a break, but please do not go South of Nowhere because a Small Wonder of Swat Kats: The Radical Squadron hosted by Sister Sister will take place. A couple of shows will be airing if you care to visit the Summerland teashop. There's no need for Suits and ties; it will be a casual affair. The shows to be shown are:

1. Superman: The Animated Series

2. Spooks

3. Super Mario World

4. Spartacus: Blood and Sand

5. SpongeBob SquarePants

6. Spartacus Vengeance

7. Steven C. Patti presents Super Robot Wars

8. The Story of Tracy Beaker

9. Suburgatory

I hope these events will meet all of your needs. It will be for all ages and is family oriented, If you have any questions and need to contact me, I will be at Sag Harbor hosting the Sword Art Online auction after 8:00 p.m.

Please ask The Suite Life on Deck bodyguard at The Harbor's main entrance on Sesame Street to call me, and I will surely Surface. Unless there was a Super Natural event that took place long ago, that causes you to ask Super Why! I will attend to you.

If you are not patient enough and go St Elsewhere, I do apologize and hope I was not Switched at Birth with Stella who is always late and blaming Skins, Slides, Soap and men.

T TV Shows in Rhymes (Graduation)

Today, The Amazing World of Gumball chronicle has just printed congratulations to the class of now, surprisingly most heard it announced on Tim and Eric Awesome Show, great job!

All Teachers will also be announcing their class and awards at the Tick, The live-action stadium at 2:00 p.m. today. Most classes have already booked and taken over to the Asylum nearby presented by T.U.F.F. Puppy and Bob

All graduates will be picked up by Turbo Charged Thunderbirds Limo Company, driven by a True Detective from Totally Spies. For safety; they will be Taken to the Teen Titans arena for assembly.

A special group will greet them upon arrival, the Trailer Park Boys from Total Drama Island, they wanted to surprise them saying it was their True Calling, Maybe?

The two principals Mr. Timon and Pumbaa will start the awards ceremony promptly at 2:20 p.m. They are known to be Two Of

A Kind after teaching Twenty Good Years, and friends from babies

The Amanda Show will televise the awards portion of the ceremony with announcers Tia & Tamera, adding a distinctive Touch during The Thick of It

Threes Company media will be the Third Watch portion of the broadcasting for people with disabilities and anyone else that has needs that will make this fit

Bang! It is 2:30 p.m. the Time Trumpet was just blown by the Thundercats of The Talk, it almost threw me out of my seat.

There will be a Total Wipe Out in awards this year, because this year the students all attended Three Rivers Academy for all Top Cat academic awards which kept them on their True Jackson VP feet

There will be four groups of Teen Titans Go! Awards, Let us begin with Ms. Taggart and her students, quiet Please! Save all noises, whistles and applauses until The Flash gives a signal time

Let's begin Class!

Our first award the Twin Peaks Scholar award goes to Maggie for her outstanding performance in Transformers Prime

The second award the Torchwood academic drama award goes to Tom for guest starring in Total Action Drama even though neither earned a Threshold dime

The Third award the Tsubasa Reservoir Chronicle award goes to Mary for outstanding athleticism in the Two And A Half Men marathon, I would need three, but it is a race

Okay that is enough! or we will be here all The Tick day sounding like Tenacious D in a Texhnolyze long-drawn-out Talesspin place

Everyone got Touched By An Angel because it suddenly came to Total Drama Action End

Oh! Did you want it to continue? Okay! We all agree it would be short, and that we can all defend

The Tyler Perry's House of Payne will host the after party at the Tron: Uprising ballroom. Tengen Toppa Gurren Lagann will be a special visitor and it will be featured on Talk Show with Spike Feresten of TechTV Vault

Newsflash! It was just announced that Tom Goes To The Mayor for a position there, remember him? He got the award earlier.

That's why am I telling you, stay afloat! I said not to listen to That Girl, she is trying to Top Gear Us, I know this is not your fault

Teenage Mutant Ninja Turtles and Taz-Mania were banned from the after party because of the things they did on The Practice; they thought it was That's So Raven.

A security guard named Titus made it Teen Wolf clear that this was not That's 70's Show and we're assuring safety to protect all Trinity Blood

A grand prize will be drawn by The Fosters who will tell some Tales From The Crypt and a Tim Man quiz will follow. The winner will join Terminator: The Sarah Connor Chronicles and Tenchi in Tokyo for a relaxing retreat and will be pampered by a Top Chef

Ah! Well hoping weather conditions are good by then; lately we heard there's lots of rain in the forecast, but certainly no flood

All good things must come to The Tudors end, so we should all remain True Blood and love Till Death

All I can say is Bravo! Everyone did it, Go Class of Now! Be a blessing to the world and the Tenchi Universe being peaceful and enduring without a fret

U TV Shows in Rhymes (Bullying)

The Upright Citizens Brigade has announced that they will be protesting at The United States of Tara courthouse in the midst of the disturbing news of bullies sending an Undercover Boss to the Ugly Betty show thinking they can torment someone by calling them an Ugly American

This will not be tolerated, since beauty is in the eyes of the beholder and "everyone is beautiful" said Judge Urusei Yatsura.

This surprising statistics is now becoming the newest form of bullying. The latest cases are as numerous as the Unsolved Mysteries, and most given the booth

Other circumstances have been featured on Untold Stories Of The ER because of their abusive nature. That is so Up and Undeclared

Nobody should be called an Ugly American much less featured and mocked on an Underdog Show

I hope that superior court Judge Utaban declare this a crime and convicts them as felons, sending them all to the The Unit of The Unsuals for a while, giving them time to contemplate that bullying is never accepted and Up to the Minute, definitely a no go!

V TV Shows in Rhymes (Celebration)

Word is out that Veggie Tales show has replaced Voltron: Defender of the Universe. It's the season's most watched show. It will be the new and upcoming feature of the week

The news was so fantastic that even The Vicar of Dibley sent a thank you note; gratitude is the only Viva La Bam they all seek

Mr. Veep, The Virginian governor also was ecstatic to join the Victorious new Vikings

Viva S Club will be presenting them with VR Tropies meaning the show rocks and is to everyone's likings

That is good news for everyone except Voltron: Defender of The Universe. They are worried about their ratings since they were number one for years, while Vanderpump Rules, Veronica Mars has ended for the season

The Venture Bros, has tried to give The Vampire Diaries, the show's competition a new producer and cast but failed in the season's lineup abruptly for no apparent reason

W TV Shows in Rhymes (Stalking)

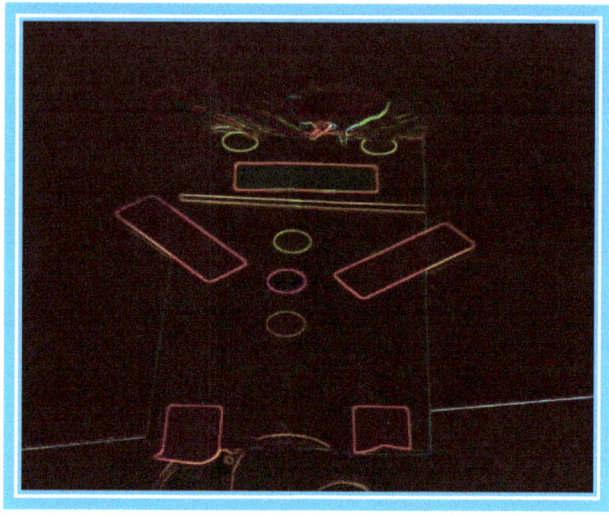

Welcome Back Kotter, I am so sorry to bother you, I know you are with The Weekenders on Waterloo Road, but I am having the Worst Week ever and it is causing War At Home

I try to hide out at Warehouse 13 at the Winx Club, but word got through The Wire and spread like Weeds and Wildfire in the Wild, Wild West

It is the person I told you about; you sometimes probe me saying "Who is it" What's My Line? I suddenly get nervous; you got the picture, a stalker by the name of Wilfred who is Wild 'N Out like When Fish Attack, looking for his Wheel of Fortune; I must confess

Would you believe? What? He hangs out in the Women's Murder Club and looks at females like they are Wonder Pets

If I was not sane, I would think he is Walking with Monsters like Wally Gator. He was banned from Women's College Basketball.

His friends The Wild Thornberrys that played Who Wants to be a Millionaire, keeps company with The Walking Dead and the W.I.T.C.H. pretending to be a White collar worker, and I need not say the rest!

The Wizards of Waverly Place told Will and Grace to take him to WWE Raw and turn him into one of the WWE Superstars of Wresting so he can win a WWE Championship Wrestling trophy to impress

I hope not me! I really do not wish him any harm, but my desire is that they make him a Wallflower on Walking The Beasts, putting up a sign at Wangan Midnight saying Wanted on arrival

Actually the Feds are on alert and Detective Wagaya No Oinari-sama will be in disguise as a Walker Texas Ranger at the Wow! Wow! Wubbzy revival

Who Pays The Ferryman? Who cares! at this point, there are other delicate issues, he gets paid somehow, and that is none of your Wonder Showzen business, we are Wipeout dealing with fear and survival

What Not to Wear! I wish I had Wings, and just cast my burdens to God asking him to keep me on The West Wing in paradise

Oh No! It is him again, behind me in the grocery store whispering: "We Can Be Heroes" Please! I will never take your corny wishes or advice

No he didn't! It is The War of the Worlds, tune into WCW Monday Nitro, at that point you'll ask What's Happening? Ask The Wendy Williams show and they will tell you; there will be Wire in the Blood. I wish for the day he becomes invisible Without a Trace

Gone are the days, when people were giants and Walking with Dinosaurs. I need one of them now to just crush him, but never mind that will partially create The World at War. I will be then fighting fire with fire, constructing something I cannot erase

I am taking a much needed vacation, with the Workaholics to reminisce on The Wonder Years near the Wonder Falls

Really! Please tell me I am not seeing him in the canoe next to me screaming "What I Like About You" Nothing but the feds in disguise, sitting in the canoe next to you. If you need an answer

Oops! There it is, Wrestling With Death, do not try to run like a prancer, answer the telephone when someone is calling

Where are my friends when I need them? What about Brian? What about Mimi? They always say to call the Whitest Kids U Know, Really! I need anyone at present.

Unexpectedly, there has been an arrest, the stalker! He has been photographed and jailed, currently featured on billboards, additionally; the news has been broadcasted at WKRP in Cincinnati and around the media world. Please! save someone from falling.

There is nothing to fear, but fear itself. Take action and protect your life and someone else's. Call your local police department if you are being stalked.

Thank you, now! Who's The Boss? Do not criticize anyone in a situation like that, unless you have journeyed on the same path they have walked.

X TV Shows in Rhymes (Equality)

For a toast to the New Year, and good things to come presently and in the future, The Xiaolin Chronicles have reviewed their X Files

They have discovered that throughout the years that only X Men have been chosen as their person of the year, so after numerous gripping pleas from X women to several correspondents and important ties

The newspaper has sided with the female generation for Xena Warrior Princess as their cover page

Xavier, The Renegade Angel is protecting everyone from further disagreements and is asking for some reconciliation at this tender stage

Now that there is no longer an X-Men Evolution but equal rights for both sexes of The X's, there is no time for either side to become XXX Holic and become vain

Currently there is peace in the land, and definitely not one person will be declared insane, or ever have to feel any more pain

Y TV Shows in Rhymes (Demonstrating)

Back in the day our ancestors told us "You Can't Do That on Television"

Well back then most of us did not even own one, so that line unquestionably needs some Yo Soy Bea revision

Never say to someone "You're The Worst" just look at your own face in the mirror and try to set an example for The Young Ones

The youths are watching and listening to you. They would like to respect you saying, "Yes Minister" and thank you for guiding them. Someday they can emulate that behavior to their daughters or sons

Now that The Young and the Restless are growing up, they will eventually get older like Yu-GI-OH and he will someday hear them saying,

To him "Yes Prime Minister" or the other way around, whatever the outcome, we are sure to model good behavior like Young Justine, that will leave them thanking you and praying.

Z TV Shows in Rhymes (Watchful)

The world will definitely come to an abrupt end. It is now looking like Zoids Chaotic Century; please do not try to climb over the highest mountain or swim under the deepest seas

Try your best to pay off all your Zombie Loan and avoid escalating fees

You will save yourself some ZEGAPAIN and your mental health will have a better forecast

Zeke and Luther please forgive and forget, in addition do not do anything you will soon regret, just leave it in the past

Now, remember that the guardian angels in Heaven are protecting you 24/7 and permanently on Zula Patrol,

Just be prepared and remember that the Devil's angels in hell are there also to devour your soul

So confess your sins and believe in The Everlasting God Almighty that will give you eternal life, so stay blessed and have some self-control.

About the Poet

Wynette McKenzie started writing poetry when she was eight years old. Her poetry is inspired by her childhood and motherhood. She is a certified Early Childhood Educator and continues to draw inspiration from her life as a Christian and her work with children.

www.ingramcontent.com/pod-product-compliance
Lightning Source LLC
Chambersburg PA
CBHW041959080526
44588CB00021B/2801